HOW TO SUCCEED IN THE ARTS... OR IN ANYTHING.

By

Ken Davenport

Davenport Theatrical Enterprises, Inc.
2017

First Printing: 2017

ISBN 978-1-365-62420-9

Davenport Theatrical Enterprises, Inc.

1501 Broadway, Suite 1304
New York, NY 10036
(212) 874-5348

kendavenport@davenporttheatrical.com

DEDICATION

This book is dedicated to my wife, who inspired me to do something I never thought in a million years I could do… get married.

If I can do that, then trust me, you can do anything.

Table of Contents

A Note From Ken

"All our dreams can come true if we have
the courage to pursue them."
- Walt Disney

Believe it or not, you've already taken one, nope, two…two steps toward whatever it is you want to accomplish… whether that's writing a show, producing a show, starting a new business, or shooting lower golf scores (oops, sorry, that's one of my personal goals that slipped in there).

You don't know what those two steps are?

First, you bought this book. You said, "I want something. And I need help doing it," and you plunked down your hard-earned cash and bought this book.

And second, <u>you're actually reading this book.</u>

That second one is a big deal, believe it or not. You know how many self-help books never get cracked open? Or how many treadmills go unused? Good intentions are just that... good. They become **great** when you do something with that intention.

And you did just that.

Already you've separated yourself from the ~~thousands~~, millions of people out there who all want to do something, whether that's in the arts or in anything, but don't do jack about it.

Or they take the first step and get that book or that treadmill and think it's going to read/or exercise itself.

Spoiler alert: It won't.

The cold, hard fact is that most people in this world are lazy. They'd rather sit on the couch, watch television, and stare at what other people are doing and say, "I could do better than that."

And then grab another handful of potato chips.

But not you. You grabbed this book instead. (Much healthier choice.)

So take a moment to congratulate yourself on the two steps you've already taken towards achieving your goal. Go ahead. Pat yourself on the back. I will wait. Are you patting? Go on, give yourself a good one. You deserve it. Because by simply getting this book and then by actually cracking it open and reading it, you've pulled ahead of the pack and are on your way to great success in the arts... or in anything.

Let's begin.

Introduction

"Nothing in this world can take the place of persistence. The slogan 'Press On!' has solved and always will solve the problems of the human race."

-Calvin Coolidge

I know a lot of successful people.

Because of what I do, and because of the success that I've been lucky enough to achieve in my life, I've found myself in the company of people who have achieved the type of success we all dream about. We're talking Tony Award® winners, Academy Award® winners, professional athletes, entrepreneurs worth hundreds of millions of dollars, famous physicians, politicians, and more.

Not only are these folks my friends, but they've also inspired me to reach higher in my own quest for success.

Tip

If you want to be a success, surround yourself with successful people. The human mind is an amazing thing, and it adapts to the environment that it's in over time. So, if you put yourself in a place where you are constantly around people with the type of success you want, whether that's artistic, financial, or even with personal relationships, slowly but surely you will adapt to that environment. Like a plant grows towards the sun, you'll find yourself leaning up to their level.

(Warning—this concept works in the reverse. Too many people I know surround themselves with individuals who are nowhere near where they want to be...and they end up sliding down to their level without even knowing it. Remember how your parents didn't want you to hang out with kids who were a "bad influence"? Turns out, they had a point.)

That's why I always look to surround myself with people smarter than I am, more creative than I am, wealthier than I am, have a better golf swing, etc. And the more of them, the better. There is strength and success in numbers.

As I surrounded myself with more and more of these successful people over the years, the more curious I got about their success. And the more comfortable with them I got, the more I poked them for details on how they got to be where they are. I've always been a curious person, but to get a chance to ask questions to people who had already achieved the kind of success that I so wanted was the biggest blessing I could ask for. It was like getting ten graduate degrees…with no tuition.

In my opinion, you can never be too curious. Or as I like to say, curiosity may have killed the cat, but it also fed the dog. ☺

I acted like a two-year-old whenever I was around any of these folks and asked them things like…

> "How did you get where you are? What were the steps you took? Did you have help? What was the best advice you ever got? What was the worst? What was the one thing you'd do differently if you were to

do it again?"

If you listen to my podcast (you can find it on TheProducersPerspective.com), you may recognize these questions...because I'm still asking them! I'm still learning with every person I meet. As long as I have something I want to do differently, or more efficiently, then I'll always be asking questions.

<u>Because you can never get an answer without first asking a question.</u>

I'd ask these questions and then...and here's the real important part...I'd shut up and listen.

TIP

The simple concept of "listening" took me a while to learn, but as one of my mentors once said to me, "Smart people talk. Smarter people listen."

I'd listen to their stories of how they started their companies, how they made it through tough times, how they made money, lost more money, and then made even more back again.

And the more I asked and the more I listened, the more I realized something about super-successful people.

It was quite an epiphany, and I remember the exact place I was when I realized it...like it was my first kiss or something! That's how important it was to me.

Are you ready for it? It may shock you, so be prepared.

The most successful people I knew...weren't the smartest people in the world.

Seriously!

We're brought up to believe that the smart ones are the successful ones (it's a teacher's trick to keep us in school studying our little butts off), but it's not always true.

While it's easy to think that only the smartest, most gifted people, the ones that are "born with it," are the ones that are the most successful, that's just not true. Not at all.

(That kind of thinking is just another excuse, or a "Limiting Belief," that keeps us on the couch, doing what we've always done, instead of getting up and taking charge of our destiny. And, it's just BS.)

> A Limiting Belief is anything we tell ourselves that holds us back from our pursuit of what we really want out of life. (e.g. "I'm not smart enough." "I'm not pretty enough." "I don't know the right people."

Just because people are gifted doesn't mean that they're going to be successful, and certainly vice versa. I remember this kid I went to high school with who aced his SATs, got A's on all his papers that he dashed off in a 50-minute study hall...and now is in a middle management job that's going nowhere. And I'm sure you know lots of folks from your youth like this too!

The fact is, success has nothing to do with smarts.

Can it help? Sure. But it ain't necessary. (That's right, people who say "ain't" can be as successful as people who can recite the Strunk & White rules from memory.)

When I learned this, man oh man, it was like breaking through the ceiling of my life. And it should be for you, too.

You don't need an IQ of 200. You don't need a law degree from Harvard. You don't need to be a card-carrying member of Mensa.

But I know what you're thinking, if it isn't smarts, then what is it that you do need to achieve the success that you've been dreaming about?

That, my friends, is what this book is about.

But if you want a clue, I think this quote says it best:

> *"Ambition wins over genius 99% of the time. Sooner or later the other guy is going to have to eat, drink, go to the bathroom, get laid or take a vacation. And that's when I catch him." – Jay Leno*

Jay Leno wasn't the best comedian when he was starting out. There were a lot of other folks funnier than he was. But

NONE who had his work ethic. And he was committed to doing something about getting better...and that's why he ended up being one of the most powerful people in Hollywood. Not because he was the most talented. And not because he was the smartest. But because he was committed.

If you're just as committed to achieving your goals, then I guarantee you can get there. All you have to do is turn the page, my friend...and do something about it.

Chapter 1: The Day That Changed My Life

This day.

This one day.

It plays over and over in my mind like a short film.

And I can remember every detail. The khaki pleated pants from the Gap I was wearing. How it was threatening to rain and I didn't have an umbrella (I never have an umbrella). How I waited for seventeen, not eighteen, but seventeen, minutes in the lobby before I got to see him. I remember everything. (That's how you know a memory is an important one, by the way. The more details you can remember, the more impact that moment had on your life.)

Before I tell you what happened when I was finally invited into His office, let me tell you how I even got to the lobby in the first place.

The legendary Director Hal Prince *(Phantom of the Opera, Sweeney Todd,* etc.*)* and winner of about 147 Tony Awards, was quoted in a very famous article in the '90s saying that Broadway no longer had any Creative Producers. Gone were the days of David Merrick, Alexander Cohen and, yep, Hal Prince (he was a Producer before he was a Director, producing the original productions of *The Pajama Game, West Side Story,* and *Fiddler on the Roof,* to name a few). Those legendary figures who knew the business and the art of the theater were gone...and what was left were big check writers. In this article, Hal longed for the days when there was that one person with a strong vision (right or wrong), with passionate ideas (good or bad), bringing people together to produce a show.

Since a Creative Producer was exactly what I wanted to be, I decided to write Hal a letter. I had been lucky enough to work with him on *Show Boat*, *Candide,* and *Parade* so I was hoping he would at least read the note...and heck, I'd be happy if he sent me an autographed photo.

So I wrote to him and said...

> *Dear Mr. Prince,*
>
> *I want to be one of those Creative Producers that you spoke about in your recent interview. That's exactly what I want to do with my life. I'm not sure how to get there, but I know it's what I want to do. Do you have any advice?*
>
> *Best,*
>
> *Ken Davenport*
>
> *P.S. An autographed photo would be awesome.*

Ok, maybe that wasn't exactly it, but you get the idea.

Well, something about the actual letter worked, because imagine my shock when I got a message on my answering machine (I told you it was the '90s) from his assistant saying that Mr. Prince would like to see me in his office at my earliest convenience.

So that's what got me into his lobby for those tense and nerve-wracking seventeen minutes.

And then...I was invited in.

And there he was. And right behind him, on an extra large super-sized shelf, were those 147 Tonys. I was as speechless as I've ever been, so he broke the silence.

"So you want to be a producer, huh?"

I nodded.

"Well, what do you want to produce?"

And with that, it was like he popped the top on a soda can that had been shaken up for a decade...

I poured out every idea I ever had for a show. Non-stop. Looking back on it, I guess it was my first pitch meeting...and I was throwing fastballs non-stop. And the pitches were all over the place...from a musical version of *Willy Wonka* to a musical adaptation of a book called *Mole People*...which is about the homeless population who live in the subway tunnels of New York City...which is probably one of the worst ideas for a musical ever! (It is a great book, though!)

I was pitching everything. After about seventeen ideas, Hal stopped me and said, "Ken, do you know the first show I produced?"

I had just read Hal's biography the day before the meeting so I'd be prepped for a question like this (it's another great read, by the way). But all that pitching took its toll. I'd had too many visions of Willy Wonka living in the subway tunnels of New York City in my head!

"No, I don't remember," I said sheepishly.

"It was *The Pajama Game*," he said.

Damn it. Of course! I knew that. But what does that have to do with *Mole People* and what I want to do? I bit my tongue and listened as Hal continued.

"Don't try to come out of the box trying to produce *West Side Story*. *West Side* was my third show. Be happy if you get *The Pajama Game*. It made money, it made people laugh...and more importantly, Ken, it got me started."

And before I could say anything else, he looked at me and he said, "Ken, just start. Produce something. Produce anything. But start. NOW."

In those few words, Hal taught me one of the most important theatrical lessons, and one of the most important *life* lessons. And it's exactly what I needed to hear, and I'd bet you the price you paid for this book that it's what you need to hear as well.

Why am I so confident that Hal's message applies to you, too? Well, look, if you bought this book, then you and I have a lot in common. I don't need to know your astrological sign to know that you're a supremely passionate person. You're an ambitious person. You're not satisfied with just sitting back and waiting for things to happen. You are always thinking about ways you could do things that would be better than the way other people are doing them. You've got a thousand ideas. And they are all good ones. You want to create great things. You want to produce shows, write books, create businesses...you want to change the world. You dream about that at night. You imagine yourself making something terrific that ripples throughout the theater community, the arts community, and maybe even the whole wide world.

And you know what? You can.

I have no doubt that there are future Lin-Manuel Mirandas reading this book. Future Steve Jobs. And yeah, future Hal Princes!

And that's exactly how you should think of yourself. You're destined for great things. You've got what it takes to be a monster success.

But...here's the challenge for people like you and people like me that Hal was getting at.

If you want to produce the next *West Side Story,* or write the next *Hamilton,* or even invent the next iPhone, you've got to remember that the people who did those things, didn't *start* with those things.

Just like *West Side Story* wasn't Hal's first show, *Hamilton* wasn't Lin-Manuel Miranda's first show. And without *In the Heights* and the zillion drafts of that show before it became a hit, he never would have written *Hamilton*. And don't even get me started on all the stuff that Steve Jobs did before the iPhone (including get fired by his own company).

You can't come out of the box trying to write or produce or design *Hamilton* or *Sweeney* or *Oklahoma!* And the same thing goes for <u>any</u> profession in <u>any</u> industry for <u>anything</u> you're trying to achieve. Sure, sometimes it does happen, and people win "the lottery" and hit it big right out of the gate. But more often it takes time and a lot of effort. When Jonathan Larson's sister accepted his posthumous Tony Award for *Rent,* she said, "It took Jonathan fifteen years of really hard work to become an overnight sensation."

Barack Obama didn't wake up one morning and say, "I want

to be President," and expect to then get elected the next year. That is impossible. First, he was a lawyer. Then a community organizer. Then a senator. He wasn't ready to be president when he graduated from college. He had stuff to learn first, relationships to cultivate, experience to gain before he could get elected and rule effectively.

I wasn't ready to produce *Willy Wonka and the Chocolate Factory* as a Broadway musical when I pitched that idea to Hal. Sure, it was a good idea, but I didn't have what was necessary to make that happen.

What Hal was trying to do was get me to do something that I could make happen on my own. He wanted me to focus on something that I could actually accomplish, because he knew that if I accomplished something small, it would put me on the path to accomplish something great.

Let me say that again…

Accomplishing something small puts you on the path to accomplish something great.

I know you want to do great things. I know you want to break barriers, bust boundaries, make billions. And I believe that you will. But don't let that stop you from starting on something that might not do any of those things for you.

What's important is to start.

I remind my consult and coaching clients of this all the time...your first show isn't your last show, it's your first show. Without it, you can't have your second show, your third, and so forth.

This was a huge concept for me to understand. And, well, to slander my own sex, it's a huge thing for a lot of young men to understand. We all come out of college or high school thinking we're the smartest people on earth and that we are going to change the world. We expect people to just hand us things because we're soooooooo smart.

And it just doesn't happen. Because we don't know half of the things we think we know. And our massive egos only look for the "big idea" that will change the world and let all the smaller ideas pass by, even though they'd get us to the big idea so much faster.

How do I know this? Because this is exactly what happened to me.

You see, there was one idea I had for a show that I didn't pitch to Hal that day. I had the idea some years before, actually, but I kept pushing it aside because I didn't feel that it was important enough. It wasn't *West Side*. It wasn't *Les Miz*. Every time I thought about it, I said, "That would be really good. Really fun. A whole lot of people would like that." But before I could do anything to make that show happen, the Big Thinker in me said, "Nah, it's not important enough."

But after Hal dropped his truth bomb in my lap that day, I went home and immediately went to work.

And bam. Just like that, my life changed.

What was the idea?

Years before, I noticed a new trend in the theatrical marketplace...the interactive show. I had seen the success of *Tony n' Tina's Wedding* and all of its 17 rip-offs including

Joey and Maria's Wedding and *Bernie's Bar Mitzvah* and *Grandma Sylvia's Funeral* and so on. And I thought, "Huh, if all these shows are successful, then this is obviously something that audiences are craving." (In hindsight, the interactive movement of the '90s was a precursor to the reality television craze, since these shows are what I call "reality theater.")

Since all of the shows seemed to take place at milestone events in people's lives (weddings, funerals, etc.), I thought, "What is another milestone event in people's lives they might want to celebrate?"

And bam...it hit me like a 1.21 gigawatt bolt of lightning into a flux capicator. What about The Prom?

That's when I came up with the idea for an interactive show set at a high school prom (which was a big-time milestone event for me and for so many of us in this country).

But, what made my show different from all the other interactive shows in the market (I'm a huge believer in differentiating yourself from the competition in order to achieve success) was that I set my show back in time...in 1989.

I wanted it to be a recreation of all my favorite '80s movies...like *The Breakfast Club* or *Pretty in Pink*...but live!

And thus, *The Awesome 80s Prom* was born.

TIP

Looking for an idea? See what is working in your market, and then use that idea as a foundation, but add your own twist to it. Like a chef does when he creates a new dish!

The Prom was a tiny Off Broadway show that ran for one night a week at the famed night club Webster Hall. It was capitalized for only $120,000. It quickly became New York's #1 Bachelorette party and Sweet 16 destination (those girls weren't even teens in the 80s)! And the show ended up running for...are you ready for this? It ran for 10 years.

It returned about 500% to its investors. And it was seen in major productions in Boston, Chicago, Minneapolis, Las Vegas, Baltimore, and even Seoul, South Korea! (And they don't even have proms in South Korea.) And now high schools do it all over the country.

And I almost didn't do it.

Because it wasn't *West Side Story*. And I wanted to produce that kind of show...a show that could earn me 147 Tonys and get me in the Theater Hall of Fame.

I didn't think *The Prom* was the type of show I wanted to be known for. I kept thinking everyone would only know me as the guy who produces a party show that gets 200 girls from Long Island drunk every Saturday night. I was more important than that, dammit!

So I kept putting it off.

And if Hal hadn't told me to just DO SOMETHING, to produce SOMETHING, I wouldn't have had one of the most professionally and personally rewarding experiences of my life.

Not only did I learn so much producing that tiny show, but I made friends that will last a lifetime (my "nerd" ended up being my Best Man at my wedding!), and it started the snowball of my career rolling down the hill.

You see, I wouldn't be here without those words from Hal. I wouldn't have an office, I wouldn't have a staff. I wouldn't have a Tony Award if it weren't for getting started on that teeny tiny idea – the one that I thought had no value. And the funny thing is, it actually had the most value...because it got me started.

So remember this as you're looking to get started in whatever it is you're doing: I don't care what you do, as long as you do something. It doesn't matter what it is, as long as you do it.

It's your first endeavor. It's not your last one.

But the truth is, Hal's inspirational words are only half of the story. They were the gas that I put in my tank. But it wasn't what got me to my goals. The real secret of this book, and the secret to your success in the arts or in anything, is what I did with those words, and how I did it.

So let's get on with it. Because you've got $#@% you want to do.

Giddy up.

Chapter 2: What's an Idea Really Worth?

Hal's magic words to me on that Thursday afternoon helped energize me and helped me focus on one specific idea.

But that's all I had. An idea.

And sure, it was a good one. Actually, I'll pat myself on the back here and say, it was a great idea! History has proven that! *The Prom* ran for ten years Off Broadway, was performed in countries all over the world, and recouped almost 500%…so I'd say it was pretty great!

But back then, when I got home from Hal's office ready to do something...anything...what was my "great idea" really worth?

Nada. Zippo. Diddly squat.

A common misconception about success is believing that it's all about a great idea. I hear people saying things like, "Oh, if only I had come up with the idea for Uber or Facebook or Post-Its! That's all I need!" Or even worse, "I *had* the idea for Uber or Facebook or Post-Its! That was my idea! And they stole it!"

The truth is, ideas are overrated. Seriously. They're worth nothing.

Ideas are vapors, thoughts, and nothing more.

I know, I can hear you all saying, "But Ken, my idea is different! I'm telling you, it's different, I've got the next Uber! It's called Schmuber! And it's so..."

Blah, blah, blah. Spare me. Your idea is worth bupkis.

You want proof? Like actual, documented, statistical, legal proof about why ideas are overrated and worth the same as that piece of lint in your pocket? Ready?

Ideas can't be copyrighted.

That's right. There is no legal protection for your "idea." The Supreme Court will not protect it…because there is no value in it.

This is a question I get from my consulting clients all the time. The conversation usually goes something like this:

"Ken, I've got a billion dollar idea. What can I do to make sure no one steals it?"

Sometimes they even ask me to sign a Non-Disclosure Agreement before they tell me what it is.

And that's when I tell them the bad news…they can't protect their idea.

This is such an important concept that it bears repeating:

Ideas can't be copyrighted.

An idea on its own, by itself, is my least favorite thing in the world. It's what I call unrealized potential.

It's like the kid with an IQ of 150 who doesn't pay attention in class.

Ugh. I can't stand <u>unrealized potential.</u>   (Just writing that makes me want to puke all over this page.)

My idea for *The Prom* was a good one. No, a great one, right?

But the fact is, without me actually doing all of the things I needed to do to make it come to life, we wouldn't even know it was a great idea.

Because it still would be just sitting there, as idle, unrealized potential.

So, the first thing I tell my clients, and the first thing I'm going to tell you, is to stop classifying ideas as good, bad, or great. They're just ideas. And the fact is...

<u>Ideas, until executed, can't be great.</u>

There are tons of great ideas out there. And I'm sure you've got a long list of ideas of things you want to create/make/accomplish.

TIP

Do you keep an actual list? You should! I keep a list of mine. And for me, they're not a list of ideas, they are a list of things "to-do"…like a grocery shopping list or things-to-fix-around-the-house. Stuff I have to cross off.

If you don't keep a list of your ideas/to-dos, start right now.

Jot 'em down. On a notepad, on your fridge, your computer, your shower door when it steams up… anywhere. But record them, because if you're like me, you're going to have so many ideas that you will forget them. Me? I put all my ideas on a "to-do" tool called Toodledo. Check it out at www.Toodledo.com. This book was once a "to-do!" And now it is a "have-done!"

Just remember, your idea list is just that. It's just a list. It's a piece of paper with words on it. Potential that must, <u>must</u>,

MUST be realized.

And guess who is going to do that? That's right muchachos and muchachettes... you.

Because if not you, who else?

It's your job... it's the artist's job... the entrepreneur's job... to put energy behind these ideas. So many people say to me, "Ken, I've got ideas, but I don't have any talent. I'm not a book writer," or, "I don't know how to make an app," or, "I don't know anything about running for political office," or whatever it is they dream about doing. And most people, because of that insecurity, stop right there. And their idea never makes it off that piece of paper, or the shower wall.

And how sad is that? (I weep for the unrealized potential!)

Because the truth is, and get ready for this one, because this is a major key in achieving the success you want...

A bad idea executed is a billion times better than a great idea sitting idle.

In your lifetime, you've probably seen a ton of bad ideas executed. Come on, you know what I'm talking about.

Surely, you've seen a bad show, a bad movie, a bad something-or-other, right?

Well, even that bad idea is 100 times better than some great idea that never gets made. A brainstorm can't do anything for anyone until it becomes an ACTUAL storm. And it's up to you to, well, ahem, "Make it rain!"

Just the other day, I heard this guy on the subway say, "I know how to fix healthcare. If only they would…" and he rambled on to his friend about how he had the answer to make health care affordable and accessible and blah, blah, blah.

After listening to him for about seven subway stops, I interrupted him and said, "Hey, those are interesting ideas, why don't you do something with them?"

That's when he shut up.

"Oh, well, who am I," he stammered. "No one would listen to

me. I can't..."

And there it was...the ultimate "Limiting Belief." He <u>can't</u>.

You know what that means, right? "I can't." Want a translation?

> **Whenever anyone says, "I can't," it means "I won't."**

The truth is you can. If you try.

The things you and I want to do are probably all reasonable things than many, many people have done before. I doubt that there's anyone reading this book because they wanted to fly to Mars and back in 24 hours, or solve some geometric equation that no one else has solved.

No. You and I want to write shows, direct shows, produce shows, get hired, etc. What we want to do isn't unprecedented. So many other people have written shows, directed shows, produced shows, gotten hired, etc.

So there is proof that it can happen! If you try.

And by saying, "I can't," you're saying, "I won't."

I won't learn how. I won't speak up. I won't try. I'd rather just talk.

And that's a shame.

Especially since I know without a doubt that if the Subway Talker just did something, anything, with his idea, that something good would happen to him as a result.

Maybe he could start a blog. Write to members of Congress. Run for office.

And even if those endeavors didn't "fix healthcare," something good would happen for him.

All entrepreneurs will tell you that even when they fail (and we fail often), there is always some kind of positive outcome that comes from "the doing," whether it's something we learn, or a new relationship, or a new opportunity. That's why you must, must, MUST (have I said that enough?) execute your ideas, regardless of how "good" you think they are…or aren't.

One of my other favorite quotes, besides the Leno quote from earlier, addresses this very subject.

When the author of *The Shawshank Redemption* and *The Green Mile* burst on the scene, he was asked how he became an "overnight success" as a screenwriter. His response?

> "There are more talented writers and directors than I working in shoe stores and Burger Kings across the nation. The difference is I was willing to put in the nine years of effort and they weren't." – Frank Daramont

That says it all, now doesn't it?

Somewhere right now, behind the counter at a McDonald's or delivering pizza for Domino's or barista-ing at Starbucks, there may be a guy with a gaggle of fantastic ideas for screenplays, Broadway shows, computer software, or, yeah, even healthcare! But if he doesn't do anything with those ideas, then he's just a guy working at a fast food joint.

And this is how so many people get "stuck" in their day jobs. They get comfortable, they get complacent...and their entrepreneurial muscles atrophy. They simply don't work! That's why you've gotta exercise 'em by doing stuff...even small stuff, like I did with *The Prom*.

What's interesting about the quote above is that I actually discovered it years ago, and have used it to inspire myself and many others.

But since then? Well, that writer went on to create a little television series that you've probably never heard of, called, *The Walking Dead*. I mean, come on, Frank! You're killing it!

Frank is a guy that kept coming up with ideas...and executing them. That's what made him a success, and it's that same exact thing that will make you a success.

I get emails from people all the time asking me what I actually do every day. "What does a producer do, Ken?" I got that question so many times that I asked 100 of my Broadway producing peers to give me a one sentence answer (which you can find on my blog at www.TheProducersPerspective.com). My one sentence answer to this common question?

"A producer's job is to make an idea happen."

But I'm going to change that just a little bit for you. Because honestly, "producer" is just another term for entrepreneur... and I believe that every artist is an entrepreneur (especially in the 21st century).

<u>YOUR job is to make an idea happen.</u>

And it *is* a job, an important one, and you have to think about it that way. You show up at a job from 10-6. You do what your boss tells you to do. And you get that @#$% done. Or don't. And then you get fired, can't pay your bills, and are miserable.

Don't let that happen!

Now, you just so happen to have chosen something, whether it's writing a show, producing a show, developing a new app, writing a book, designing a new line of office furniture. I don't care what it is, but you are hiring yourself to do that specific thing. And your job, should you wish to accept it (and if you're reading this book I know you are), <u>your job is to make</u>

that idea <u>happen</u>.

Sound scary?

It's not. It's incredible. Because, just imagine what can happen to you when that idea gets made? The money, the fame, the respect, the love, <u>the everything</u>...all because you executed an idea.

And I'm going to help you make the execution easier, so it takes less effort than you think.

Read on.

Chapter 3: How to Make an Idea Happen (It Ain't As Hard As It Sounds)

"It is by acts and not by ideas that people live."
- Anatole France

So if we have an idea, how do we get it to become a reality? How do we achieve success in our chosen field? How do we make that thing happen?

Big question, right?

Let's try to make it a little easier.

Whenever I try to figure out big, heady, life-altering stuff like this, I think back to The Princeton Review SAT class I took when I was in high school. What they taught us was that to find the right answer to a problem, you start by eliminating the wrong answers.

So that's what we're going to do!

We're going to start getting to where we want to go by crossing off what we know doesn't necessarily apply.

We know that success is *not* necessarily about talent. Sure it's great to be super talented, smart, and all those things... but it isn't a requirement in order for you to achieve success, fame, money, or whatever it is you want. So eliminate that like it was a possible answer on those SATs. Out it goes.

We also know that success is not about the "perfect" idea. You don't have to have the next *Hamilton* or the next Uber to be successful. Sure, it helps if you've got the most unique invention to hit the planet since the wheel or the remote control (what did we do before those!?), but that doesn't mean you'll find success.

So if it's not those things, what makes something or someone a success? What is the key? What is *the secret?*

The secret is this…

<u>To achieve success in the arts or in anything, you have to take action.</u>

Whatever you want to do, no matter what it is, action is the gas that you must put in your tank. Without it, your idea will be nothing more than that worthless vapor just waiting, impatiently, to be ignited by action.

TIP

For us in the theater biz, this concept is very easy to remember because there is an "act" in "action." So if you are ever in doubt or stuck and find yourself saying, "I can't get beyond this, I don't know what to do," remember, put the "act" in "action." (If you're a Hollywood type, then you can think, "Lights! Camera! ACTION!")

Sounds easy, doesn't it? It is! Or it will be when you're finished with this book. Because over the next several chapters I'm going to reveal the tips and tricks you can use to take the action necessary to achieve all the things you want to achieve.

But it is that simple. In fact, I think of accomplishing something…anything…like the instructions you get on a shampoo bottle. Have you ever read those? They go something like this:

SHAMPOO INSTRUCTIONS

1. Lather

2. Rinse

3. Repeat

Achieving anything you want in life is as easy as washing

your hair. (How's that for a sound bite, huh? I should put that on a t-shirt or sell it to "successories.")

But it is true.

Once you figure out what that thing is that you want to accomplish…create a new line of office furniture, develop an app, write a show, become president, shoot scratch golf (that's one of my big ones!)…all that you need to do is break it up into smaller, one mile at a time, bite-sized action items, or those simple "to-dos" we talked about earlier.

And when I say simple, I mean simple, like picking up the dry cleaning or calling your mother.

The reason you have to break down your goals into these smaller, easily actionable items (Or EAIs, as I call them) is that most often, your goals are ginormous! Just the idea of writing a play, winning a Tony award, shooting a movie, or opening a restaurant can seem so big, so overwhelming and therefore so difficult to accomplish that the initial response of our brain is to say, "What am I crazy? No way! That's too difficult. I'm not going to do that! Because I CAN'T!" (And we all know what that CAN'T word means!)

We all have this inner voice...this insecure, frightened and yep maybe even a bit lazy, inner voice that gets in the way of us accomplishing our goals.

You know what I'm talking about, right? Don't worry, you're not alone. We all have this evil butthead of a character inside of us. I know I do! You know how long I sat on the couch before getting up to write this chapter? You know how I finally did it? I told myself, "Just write one page. Just one page and then you can go back and watch another episode of *SVU*."

One page didn't seem so difficult. And when I finished I'd have Benson and Stabler waiting for me as my reward.

So I got up to write one page.

And ended up writing ten.

When you chunk up your larger goals into simpler, easier tasks instead of a giant monstrosity, your mind finds it much easier to process. So instead of setting a goal to finish a play, your first goal might be to just come up with an idea for a play. And then your next goal might be to come up with a list of characters in the play. And then maybe write the first setting...not even the first scene...just the setting!

All of these things are much easier to achieve. And that hard-to-tame inner voice instead says, "Ok, that I can do... and then I can get back on the couch."

And what happens is, soon enough, you trick your mind by doing so many of these smaller actions that you've accomplished your larger goal, without that lazy part of you even knowing!

And, there is nothing more fulfilling then accomplishing a goal, right? Think about those moments in your life that you've done something you worked hard to achieve. It feels awesome, right?

Well, when you set these smaller, and easier to crush, mini-goals, you get that feeling more often! And that energy helps push you into the next one.

The human mind is fueled by the pain-pleasure principle. We search out pleasure. We avoid pain. Work is pain. Which is why we'd rather sit on a couch. But there's LESS pain when the work is simpler...and MORE pleasure, because we'll accomplish more small goals along the way.

This process works especially well not only when you are struggling to get started because you want to watch the *SVU* marathon that just started, but also when you need to do something that you may not know how to do. Whenever you're heading into unchartered territory, the fear intensifies the body and mind's desire to do nothing. Not only is getting off the couch work, but it's also scary work that could lead to embarrassment and failure because you've never done it before!

It's easier to get off the couch to do something you do every day (which is why I'm a big fan of creating habits—e.g. writing at the same time every day, limiting TV (aka *SVU*) time to a specific number of hours per night, etc.). If you jumped out of a plane every day for a year, it'd be pretty easy by the time the 366th day came around. But getting off the couch to jump out of a plane when you've never jumped before? Yikes!

Our body has a psychological and physiological reaction to anything we haven't done before by saying, "You can't do that. You shouldn't do that. You don't know what will happen!" And when that something we're trying to do is something big, well, just forget it! It's like thinking about running a marathon. That's 26.2 miles. No way can I run that far. No way.

But, if I take that 26.2 miles and chop it up into little pieces and start one at a time...by say, running just a half a mile today. And a full mile tomorrow. And then two miles next week. And so on. Before you know it, you're up to marathon distance without even realizing it. Because you've done it one chunk at a time. You've eased into the giant-sized goal, and tricked your brain and your body into running the marathon.

A lot of people talk about achieving these kinds of goals by saying you must "break out of your Comfort Zone." Honestly,

I hate that phrase, because I find that anyone who tries to break out of anything, gets busted. Breaking out is violent, and is too jarring on the mind and body.

What you need to do is s t r e t c h your Comfort Zone, a little bit every day, just like stretching any muscle. You don't say, "I'm going to do a split," and then just force your legs down to the ground. You'll break your you-know-what.

No. You stretch a little bit every day, and you get there without knowing how you got there. And the same is true with your Comfort Zone. You stretch it and stretch it until it gets bigger...and you're comfortable doing those bigger things!

You don't want to get rid of your Comfort Zone. You just want it to be the size of the entire planet.

How do you stretch it? How do you expand it?

One little actionable item at a time.

And like I said before (actually I said it twice before so you know it's crucial) creating small actionable items to check off your list is so much MORE important when you're doing something that you haven't done before.

Let me give you a specific example of this concept, by going back to the story of how I created and produced my very first show.

If you remember, I came home from that meeting with Hal Prince all jazzed up and energized and ready to do... something, right? Anything. And I had this idea, but it was still just that idea. A worth nothing, car without gasoline, idea, called *The Awesome 80s Prom*. I knew it could work, but honestly I had no idea how to make it happen. None. The idea of creating a show, any show, was overwhelming. How could I put this all together? Where would I start? I didn't know... <u>because I'd never done it before!</u>

When I got home from my inspiring meeting with Hal, I sat there at my desk, with my idea and nothing else. And I sat there for hours, thinking about the giant task ahead of me of creating a show.

I finally got moving when I STOPPED focusing on that giant

concept. I stopped thinking about the final outcome. I didn't think about opening night or the 10th anniversary or me winning awards. I didn't focus on finishing the marathon. I focused on just getting out of the starting blocks.

But how?

I quieted my mind and said, "Ok, this is going to be an interactive show. It is going to be improvised. And that means I need actors. Because actors improvise. Ok, ok. I need actors."

Now here's a little thing about me. I'm just a wee bit OCD (shocking, right?). If you've ever been into my office for a consult or a coaching session, then you probably noticed that my desk is perfectly clean. I actually can't leave my office or go to bed at night until there's nothing on my desk. Whatever gets put there during the day, I have to finish before the end of the day. Or I don't go home.

So I used that idea and said to myself, "If I post an audition notice in Backstage looking for actors then I'll get a ton of submissions." (There's never a shortage of actors in New

York City.) "My mailbox will be filled with pictures and resumes of people wanting to be a part of my project. And then those submissions will sit on my desk. And then I'll have to do something with them!"

And just like that I had Action Item/To Do #1 – POST AUDITION NOTICE.

To be honest, I didn't even know what that next step after getting those pictures and resumes was! But I didn't focus on it. I knew I'd figure it out, because God knows I couldn't have anything sit on my desk for more than a day. I used that personality quirk of mine as a *trigger*, a way to start the snowball of this idea rolling down the hill.

Posting an audition notice was the first, and most important, action, because it started the momentum.

TIP

What triggers do you have in your personality that can kick you into high gear? Look at what makes you tick and use that to get yourself going.

And what happened next? Just like I predicted, the submissions came pouring in, filling up my mailbox (this was before the days of email — and by the way, now I'm just as OCD about my email inbox as I am about my desk — I can't go to bed until my inbox is empty and "actioned").

I put all the pictures and resumes on my desk and stared at them in their 10 x 12 manila envelopes.

"Well, I guess the next step is to open them." (Action #2)

So I did.

And then I thought, "Well, I guess I should separate them into two piles, the ones that I think are good for this project, and the ones that aren't right."

So I did. (Action #3)

I took the "not right" pile and filed them away for possible future projects, leaving the pile of the actors I was interested in staring at me on the desk.

"I guess I should audition them."

So I booked a room at a rehearsal studio, and we had auditions. (Action #4)

Then I had to decide which actors I liked and have them back in for callbacks. (Action #5)

Then I had to pick the ones I liked for my final cast. (Action #6)

And wouldn't you know it, I had a cast! All because I started an action sequence with one little audition notice on Backstage.

One thing led to the next led to the next…like dominoes, or computer code.

But I didn't stop there.

Once I had a cast, I had to have a rehearsal.

Now, it's important to know that at this point, <u>I still had no idea what the show was going to be!</u> I knew that it was going to be about the 80s, at the Prom, and that it was going to have a cast of characters similar to the characters in all those John Hughes movies. Oh, and I knew it was going to have a lot of improv. But it wasn't like I was some big improvisational expert! In fact, 30 minutes before the first rehearsal for *The Awesome 80s Prom*, I was at a McDonald's around the corner from the rehearsal studios reading a book called *How to Improv!*

Seriously!

I may not have known exactly what I was going to do, but the point is...<u>I was doing.</u>

And sure, it was scary...but in a very short period of time, I had taken a worthless, nothing idea sitting idle in my brain, and gotten a whole bunch of people together in a room ready to make it a reality.

And how did I get there?

I had a list of To-Dos, of small *Easily Actionable Items*, like doing the laundry, or making an appointment to get your hair cut, etc. Except mine were posting an audition notice, opening envelopes, having auditions, scheduling a rehearsal, etc. Each one led to the next, like a chain.

And the great thing about taking these small but important steps is that they have a way of increasing the speed and energy of your overall action.

As I've mentioned, there's no question that the first action you take is the hardest, but it's also the most important one. Why? Because it sets the others in motion.

It's like pushing a small snowball down a hill.

Over time, that snowball is going to gain weight, and speed, and momentum. And pretty soon, it'll be chugging down that hill so fast, you won't be able to stop it if you tried.

That first rehearsal led to a second and then a third and it eventually led to me saying, "Okay, I now have a show. I have to find a theater."

And by the time I found that theater, the snowball was speedin' so fast it didn't come to a halt until ten years later when *The Prom* ended its run in New York City.

And I know you're like, "Ten years later?! It just happened?"

Well, yes. That's exactly what it felt like.

When you take your mind off the big, monstrous goals, and just focus on the next small thing you need to accomplish, you'll find that you'll eventually reach that big goal and not even realize how you got there.

I couldn't have imagined that one day I'd be in Seoul, South Korea watching a cast of Koreans perform *The Awesome 80s Prom*. But that never would have happened without me posting that very first audition notice years earlier.

If I had gone home after that meeting with Hal and said, "Ok, I want to create a show that gets licensed to high schools all over the country and is performed in Korea," the show never would have happened.

You don't accomplish big goals by focusing on the big goal.

You accomplish a big goal by forgetting about it, and focusing on small ones instead.

This isn't only true for artists trying to achieve "big" things. This is also true for businesses (Mark Zuckerberg was only trying to create a site to check out freshman girls at Harvard when he created Facebook).

It's even true for physicians.

When I was shooting a documentary a few years ago (something else that I had never done before that moment and had to figure out along the way), I spoke to one of the top cancer researchers in the country and asked him about his battle against such a challenging disease.

"How do you go about curing cancer," I asked.

He told me the one thing he did NOT do was wake up every morning and say, "I'm going to cure cancer today."

If he did, he'd probably never get out of bed, because that

concept is such an enormous and challenging task. Like David facing a Goliath but ten times bigger and more dangerous.

Is this doctor on his way to curing cancer? Yes! He sure is. But it's one experiment at a time. One trial. One test case. One actionable item at a time.

I also spoke to singer-songwriter Edwin McCain, who wrote the big hit, "I'll Be," which was #5 on the *Billboard* charts, appeared in a Disney movie, on television, and in thousands and thousands of weddings around the country.

I asked him how he wrote such a successful song, and he said to me, "Anyone who tells you they sit down and write a hit song is a liar. You just sit down and write one word at a time."

He had NO idea that "I'll Be" would take him from performing in front of a twenty or so people in a dingy bar to twenty thousand people in a giant stadium.

Of course that's what he wanted, and maybe even dreamed

about, but he didn't think about it when he was writing that song. He got there by focusing on writing "one word at a time."

And that's how it is done. It's how anything is done. One word at a time. One note at a time. One step at a time.

Success is about simple actionable items. That's why at the end of all of my consult and coaching sessions, I always give my clients three action items to work on over the next 30 days. I break it down and say, "Look, here are three things to do. Only three. You do these things, you will be closer to your goal. Guaranteed."

How can I say this?

I know it works not only because of *The Awesome 80s Prom*, but because of everything else I've done in my life and career, from that first show, to the documentary I just mentioned, to making a board game, to so much more.

I find an action item to start the process, and then I find another. And then another and another and another.

What's the one thing I can do to start the *Prom* ball rolling? What's the one thing I can do to produce *Spring Awakening* on Broadway?

Or to develop a Broadway board game?

Wait...you don't know about *Be A Broadway Star,* the only Broadway Board Game on the market?

Oh, then you gotta hear this story.

Here's how it came to be...

One night, my then-girlfriend (now wife) came home from a theater-people party one night and I asked her if she had fun.

"Oh yeah. We played a board game called *Apples to Apples*," she said.

That made no sense to me.

I remember thinking, "*Apples to Apples*? Why aren't all these Broadway fans playing a <u>Broadway</u> board game?"

And then I realized they didn't play one...because there wasn't one.

So I vowed to make one!

I even remember coming up with the title in the shower..."*Be A Broadway Star!*" I wrote it in fog on the shower door.

A great idea, right?

Sure, but if I didn't action it, it would have fogged over fast, and like all ideas without action, just disappeared.

You know what my first action item was? Are you ready?

It was...

"Google how to make a board game."

☺

And wouldn't you know it, I found an article.

I started there, and one step at a time I developed a game that is now one of the best-selling Broadway gifts on Amazon.com.

It seems simple, doesn't it? Almost too simple, right?

Isn't that a good thing? When something simple actually works?

Because this concept surely does.

In fact, it can't <u>not</u> work. No matter what your goal is.

I can't guarantee how fast you'll get there, no one can. But I guarantee if you keep doing @#$% every day to make whatever it is you want to make happen, you will absolutely succeed.

How can I guarantee it?

Because this strategy isn't just self-help BS.

It's science.

CHAPTER 4: LET'S GET PHYSIC-AL ABOUT SUCCESS

> "SUCCESS IS A SCIENCE; IF YOU HAVE THE
> CONDITIONS, YOU GET THE RESULT."
> - OSCAR WILDE

Ok, I can tell, you want some proof, right?

Proof that the stuff I'm yapping about will work?

Of course you do. Because you and I are alike. We like to know the things we invest our time and money in are going to work.

You want proof.

Like real live, MIT like, factual, dependable proof that the ideas I'm talking about work.

Then let's talk physics. Yep, I said it. Physics.

I know, you hated Physics. Or maybe you didn't even take it when you were in school (I avoided it like I avoid doing musicals about vampires). But bear with me. This will be a lot easier than it sounds.

First, before we get all scientific equation-like, let's back up a step . . .

What I did to create and produce *The Awesome 80s Prom*, which, by the way, is the same technique I used to crowdfund *Godspell* (my attorney told me seven times it was impossible), and livestream *Daddy Long Legs* (people still ask me how I "did it"—I sometimes have to make it sound more difficult than it was), and develop that board game I talked about in the last chapter, is the same strategy I used to accomplish anything I've wanted to do in my life...including write this book.

You already know that that the first thing I do is break the giant task into smaller ones. I think of it like cutting up a steak. You can't digest the whole steak in one bite, right?

74

You couldn't even fit it in your mouth. And if you could, you'd either choke or get super sick.

So what do you do? You cut it up, chew it thoroughly, and digest it...say it with me...one bite at a time. Think of success the same way...it's eating big steaks one bite at a time. That big task you want to accomplish gets chopped up and chewed on, one piece at a time.

Now that you have that reminder, let's go back and really look at those small items I actioned for *Prom*. What was the first thing I did? I posted that audition notice. That was Action #1. Why did I start there? Because I knew if I posted that notice, then people would respond to it.

How did I know that would happen?

Science.

Or, yep, that class we loved to hate (or just didn't take!)...Physics.

More specifically, it's Newton's Third Law of Motion.

<u>For every action there is an equal and opposite reaction.</u>

Don't you love how the word "Action" is in that law? I do!

For *Prom*, my action was to post an audition notice. The *reaction* was that people submitted their resumes.

One of my next actions was to call the actors in for an audition. They *reacted* by showing up. And so on and so on. Action and reaction. Action and reaction. Energy, energy, energy!

This is what the universe does, <u>and it does so immediately</u>. The moment you start actioning your tasks, the universe wakes up and starts working with you to make them happen! All you have to do is add energy to your dreams, your wants, your desires through actual tasks, and the universe has no choice but to respond. It's part of nature's laws. It's Newtonian physics.

<u>Every action has a reaction.</u>

This is why you can't just "think" your way to success (which we'll get to later), but you have to actually do something about it. And once you commit to that action, there's that reaction, and then you action again, and all of a sudden you're in an action-packed tennis match. Back and forth, back and forth, accomplishing more and more, faster and faster. It's just up to YOU to start the process with that initial action, or initial trigger.

Or, to continue with the tennis analogy (and get away from scary physics), this process is what I call "serving the tennis ball," and it's what all artists and all entrepreneurs do. They serve the ball. They start the game. And they wait for someone to hit that ball back. And if someone doesn't, they serve it up again, and again, and again.

This is what I do every day, all day long! I make calls, inquire about rights, ask people to invest, advertise, etc. I serve. I start the game. **I take action.** And wait for the reaction.

And then I'm ready to hit that ball back again...until I win. ☺

That's why your job, whatever it is you want to do...produce a musical, write a play, open a restaurant, build an app...is to serve the ball, start the snowball down the hill, tap the first domino, light the match, etc., etc. I could come up with a thousand analogies like that.

But said more simply...it's your responsibility to start the action. Science will take care of the rest.

And, as I mentioned briefly in the last chapter, what's terrific about this strategy is that once you start, it's easier to keep going. Your actions and reactions tend to pick up speed and momentum as you continue down the road of accomplishing your goals.

Why is that?

Guess. Go on. GUESS!

Yep, it's science!

Let's go back to our good friend Newton! Let's take a look at his First Law of Motion:

An object in motion tends to stay in motion.

Ever say to yourself, "I don't want to write today," or even "I don't want to get out of bed?" Don't worry. We all have.

But, if you manage to crawl yourself to the computer and start to write, and those words start to flow, you can't seem to stop? And the more you type, the faster and faster you seem to go?

You do, right?

Or what about going to the gym? You wake up in the wee hours of the AM, and the thought of putting on clothes and jumping on a treadmill makes you want to crawl back deep under your covers and hide. Right?

But let me guess...once you get on that treadmill, and get moving, with your blood pumpin' and your energy flowin', you're happy you did, because you feel better *and* because you're proud of overcoming your resistance. Right?

No matter what your task, once you're in it, it just seems to happen. That's because physics and science have taken over.

All you have to do is get yourself started, because...**the key**

to success is getting yourself in motion in the first place.

And I won't lie. Starting is the hardest part. That's why I also urge my clients to make sure that first action, the one that gets you going, is a small one...an easy one...something that doesn't take a lot of effort (e.g. Google how to make a board game).

If the first action is too challenging, you might find yourself never getting started. That's why trainers make your first day of exercise pretty simple - to get you moving...literally!

TIP

When starting a new project, make your first action an easy one.

Start with a small action, wait for the reaction, and keep yourself in motion.

And get this! What's incredible about this "physic-al" process is that the more you do it (action, reaction, action, reaction, object-in-motion-staying-in-motion), the more powerful your actions become.

Seriously!

The more you commit, the greater the results.

Why?

No, not science.

Even better.

MATH!

OK, I know. It's hard to get excited about math, so we'll make it about math and...money. That'll cheer you up. ☺

Do you know what Compound Interest is?

> Compound Interest is interest added to the principal of a deposit or loan so that the added interest also earns interest from then on.

Compound Interest is a fancy way of explaining why $10,000 over 10 years at 10% interest equals $25,937.42, not $20,000.

In other words, interest earns interest. Interest _compounds._

And what's exciting is that action compounds in the exact same way that interest compounds! Action breeds action. The more you take action, the more results you get.

I was reminded of this when I was flying back from London recently. I had a big keynote speech to deliver at an event, and I had practiced it three times already, so I decided to take a little break and watch _The Martian_ with Matt Damon.

At the end of the _The Martian_, Matt Damon's character, who (spoiler alert!) just got off Mars, says this about the possibility of dying on the planet...

> _"You can either accept that or you can get to work. That's all it is—you just begin, you do the math, you solve one problem then you solve the next one and then the next and if you solve enough problems you get to come home."_

Bingo.

So, whatever it is that you want to do...start. Take that first action. Solve that first problem. Serve that tennis ball!!!

And let science help you get to your next action. And your next. And your next.

It's inevitable.

You'll be amazed at how quickly you make progress, without even realizing it.

And all because of subjects you hated in high school. They'll be your favorite subjects soon enough.

Chapter 5: Why The Secret is BS (Sort Of)

> "You are the masterpiece of your own life.
> You are the Michelangelo of your own life.
> The David you are sculpturing is you."
> - Dr. Joe Vitale

In 2006, a book hit the market that revolutionized the self-help market. It was called *The Secret*.

Why did it cause such a ruckus?

Because Oprah pimped it out.

Yep, the most powerful salesperson on the planet held what

was the equivalent of an infomercial on her show about *The Secret* and books went flying off the shelves like tickets to *Hamilton*.

In case you missed that episode or the subsequent hubbub, *The Secret* tells its readers that if they are grateful for what they have, and think positively about what they want, they will literally attract those things right to their doorstep. See checks arriving in your mailbox? Poof, there they are. See yourself meeting your soulmate? There she is!

Sounds easy, right? Well, that's why it was such a successful book! Everyone is looking for the easiest route to love and riches and success. And this book promised it.

In a way, *The Secret* is a classic "get rich quick" scheme, because the process it promotes requires minimal effort. And who wouldn't plunk down $20 for a book or DVD that told you an easy way to get everything you want. I certainly did!

The irony of the success of this book is that it is based on a principle that has been taught for hundreds and hundreds of years called "The Law of Attraction." It was just repackaged in a more commercial presentation, given a much better title (people want to know "secrets," they don't want to know "laws") and bam, it made a billion dollars.

A better interpretation of the Law of Attraction is in the classic Napoleon Hill book, *Think and Grow Rich*, which was one of the first books to take this concept and describe how to apply it to your life and to your eventual success. (I'd read this one before *The Secret,* if you want to learn more about The Law – it offers some very specific action items that you can execute to make things happen for you in your life.)

And, let me say that, without a doubt, the Law of Attraction does work.

Then why do I think *The Secret* is BS?

Ok, maybe BS is a strong couple o' words (or letters, in this case, since I'm trying to keep this family friendly). The truth is, it's not BS. Like I said, I own a copy and make sure I read it every year.

Being grateful and thinking positively about the things you

want in your life, whether that's a Tony Award, a million dollars, or a significant other, are super important in getting any one of those things. But where *The Secret* comes up short is by suggesting that merely thinking about what you want is enough. It isn't. It's just half of the work.

You have to put those thoughts, and all that positive energy to work, and take specific steps towards those goals.

(In fact, isn't that what the author of *The Secret* did? She may have dreamed about millions of dollars arriving in her mailbox, but until she wrote down what *The Secret* was, until she conducted interviews about it, until she had the book designed, published, etc., she wasn't going to earn a penny. She took action to make her desires happen.)

Let's say you want to climb a mountain. You don't stand in front of a mountain dreaming, "I want to be at the top of this mountain," and think you'll magically be transported to the top, do you?

No, you say, "I want to get to the top of this mountain," and then you summon the energy and the will to climb it, one step at a time. And then, before you know it, you're at the summit, looking down at where you started, thinking, "Wow. Look what I did!"

We now know that there is no quick way to success. Sorry, folks, but the only way to guarantee that you get that Academy Award or make a million bucks is through work...and through action...and a heck of a lot of it!

Does that mean you should throw your copy of *The Secret* away? Absolutely not. **Gratitude** and **Positive Thinking** are essential parts of success, but they are just only the first half of what you need to do to get where you want to go.

It's like the prologue for your journey towards success.

Here's why...

Remember how I said that the hardest thing about taking action is getting started?

Well, it's a heck of a lot easier to get moving when you've got positive thoughts flowing through your brain. When you can put yourself into a positive state, feeling like you can accomplish anything, feeling confident, feeling attractive, etc. it's so much easier to pick up that phone, send that email, write that first chapter, ask someone out...whatever you want to do! It's just easier to accomplish when you're thinking positively.

So yes, use *The Secret* to get you pumped and primed...for action.

Because that's what is necessary.

This is what *The Secret* doesn't tell you and why its success irks me a bit. The author of *The Secret* hopes and dreams that you'll take the action you need *because* you're in that positive state.

When the truth is, it's the reverse. <u>The action is the important part.</u> The action is where things get done. The action is where success happens. The positive state just helps propel you to action. It's the springboard for success.

But unless you do something with that positive state, you're just going to be a happy-go-lucky, smiling drifter who loves puppies and rainbows.

So why didn't *The Secret* tell you about the "Action" phase of making your dreams come true?

Because that's the hard part.

Thinking is easy. Standing in your shower and coming up with ideas for board games or interactive shows or whatever it is...shoot, that's the easy part. I bet you've got a thousand ideas. I bet you've got lots of things on your list that you want to accomplish. Personal goals. Professional goals. Probably even goals for other people. Thinking about them, dreaming about them, imagining them coming true...anyone can do that. Doing something about them requires energy, sweat, effort. And NOT everyone can do that.

Only a very small percentage of the population can (and you're part of that group, by the way).

You think *The Secret* would have sold as many books if Oprah got up and said, "To lose weight, make money, write a novel, you've got to work your butt off starting right this very second." No way. They sold books because they said, "Just think about it and it will happen."

The Secret tapped into the unfortunate truth about the majority of people in the world. They are lazy! They literally want to think, "Oh, I can imagine my way to making millions and millions of dollars." The fact is, you can't.

What you can do is think and imagine your way to feeling so positive and so good and so confident that you step up and do things that you never would have done *without* being in that state. You are grateful for what you have, and you are thrilled about where you are headed. You are the perfect candidate for success.

And yes, being in that state is a necessary component of taking the action that this book, and your work, requires. But it's just phase one. It's the first step. It's the preparation. It's like the plié before the pirouette.

So the real "secret" is...positivity is what lights the fuse of your action...but it's the action that makes things blow up.

Chapter 6: How to Create a Plan for Your Success

"Planning is bringing the future into the present so that you can do something about it now."
- Alan Lakein

Alright, so we know what it takes to achieve success.

But where do we start?

Having tools in a toolbox doesn't build a house. You've got to take out those tools and put them to use.

And, you need a blueprint...a plan...to put those tools to use.

This chapter is about exactly that - how to create a very simple, easy to follow and easy to execute plan on how you can start your journey to your success immediately.

I don't want you just *thinking* about your goals and ambitions, I want you doing something about it, as soon as effin' possible!

So here's how you start...with a three-step plan that's guaranteed to set you off on the right path.

Are you ready?

Here goes.

_____'S

(your name here)

3-STEP PLAN FOR SUCCESS

STEP 1: Decide what you want to do.

Do you want to produce a show? Do you want to write a show? Do you want to be president, or do you want to open a restaurant? Lose 20 lbs? Learn Spanish? Drop 5 strokes off your golf handicap? It doesn't matter what it is, it just matters that you decide to do it.

Do you have it?

Great, write it down here.

I WANT TO _____

And now, just like a character in any great play, you have an objective. And just like those heroes you love to watch in plays, or movies, you are going to be that hero and pursue that goal no matter what obstacles get in your way. Right?

That's Step 1. Easy, right?

So, on to the next.

STEP 2: Pick one action, any action, that gets you closer to your goal.

Now, this is important. I don't care what the action is. It can be anything, but I strongly suggest that it be a small, simple to execute "to-do" or what I call in my office an EAI or *Easily Actionable Item* (as you've heard me refer to in this book).

EAIs get crossed off the list quickly and give you an immense feeling of accomplishment...and they make you want to complete another one. An EAI can be as simple as calling a Publisher about the rights to a book... or even simpler... googling the Publisher for their phone number... and then the next day's EAI can be to call that Publisher! Easy right?

Does this concept make sense? If not, go back and read this page again because it's super important.

Start simple so you can guarantee that you'll accomplish it. Remember, an object in motion tends to stay in motion, so let's get you moving, which will get you motivated.

Write that action item down here:

MY ACTION ITEM IS TO: _____

Got it all written down?

Awesome. Now, the next step is, uh, duh, do it.

Don't think. Just do. (Yep, *Star Wars* fans, that was my Yoda impersonation.)

I don't want you saying, "But what if they say no?" or "What if

I get a voicemail?" or "What if I can't find it?" or "Oh no, they'll never let me do this?" or any limiting belief like that. Just do it. No questions, no doubt...NO THINKING! Just doing.

Remember what Shakespeare himself said...

> *"Our doubts are traitors, and make us lose the good we oft might win, by fearing to attempt."*
>
> *- Measure for Measure*

Shakespeare was a playwright (unless you believe the conspiracy theories), and I'm sure he faced his own doubts and insecurities all the time. He was human. But he found a way to beat them.

I think the trick is to pretend you are NOT human.

You want to become a machine. Machines can't doubt. They can only do what they are programmed to do.

You want to be like a robot. "I do action. Beep bop blip. I do action."

Thinking too much can actually paralyze you into a state of inaction. So don't!

Did you do it? Then on to step three.

STEP 3: Repeat Step 2.

You saw that one coming didn't you. Good, then you're already catching on. What you want to do is create an "Action Loop" in your plan. Complete one, come up with another, and complete that new one. Then come up with another, and complete that one, and so on and so on.

Step 3 reminds me of when I wrote computer programs in Basic on my TRS-80 computer in 1981. They'd look something like this:

> *10 New*
> *20 Print "I love musicals."*
> *30 Go to 20*

And the program would fill the screen with, "I love musicals," over and over and over and over. And it would NEVER stop!

It was an endless loop. You'd have to "break" the program to get it to quit.

You're programming your mind to do the same thing. With Step 3, you're creating a non-stop action loop that will just keep repeating itself over and over until you achieve what you want to achieve. And, by that point, you'll probably be on to your next goal! And since you'll have become such an action-oriented machine, you'll be crushing that one too.

That's it! An easy-peasy three step plan that gets you moving today towards your goals.

Now look, you will hit some trouble spots along the way, without a doubt.

Complications arise, both personal and professional. Stuff gets in front of your snowball that's rolling down the hill that tries to derail it off course. Don't worry, the more you do, the more action and energy you put into your project, the faster that project gets going, and the more momentum you have to roll right over whatever is in your path.

It's physics again!

But still, you'll hit some patches that pose some problems. That's why in the next chapter I'm going to give you some tips on how to get through them and push on, instead of giving up.

Because that just ain't an option.

Chapter 7:
Troubleshooting On The
Road to Success

"If they don't let you in the front door,
go down the chimney."
- James L. Nederlander

What do you do when you get stuck?

First, you must acknowledge that you're stuck. It's OK. It happens. To everyone! Some of man's greatest accomplishments were derailed at one point or another, from the pyramids to the Great Wall of China to Uber, and Google, and everything in between...including just about every show I've ever produced.

This is especially true in the entertainment industry thanks to its collaborative nature. You need many, many people to make a musical or a film. The more people who are involved, the more stumbling blocks you're going to encounter.

It's a fact. So prepare for it. And you <u>will</u> get beyond it.

So don't panic. Don't say, "I quit." Just take a breath and say, "I'm stuck! And now I'm going to *do* something to get unstuck."

Because there is always something you can do. There is always an action to take.

Here are a few suggestions to help get you through those moments when you find it hard to take action, whether that's because of things beyond your control, or just because, well, you're tired! Actioning is a ton of work. It can be exhausting.

Here are a few ways to work through what super-blogger Seth Godin calls *The Dip* (read his book for further reading on this subject):

1. <u>Discover your Personal Action Triggers (P.A.T.)</u>

A Personal Action Trigger is something specific to your personality that helps get you going. For example, I told you about my slightly-neurotic-yet-it-works-for-me OCD need to have my desk totally clean by the end of the day. I knew that if I had a pile of pictures and resumes on my desk, staring at me (literally!), that I'd HAVE to do something about it. That was my PAT.

We all have them. And it can be anything. It can be that you work better with rap music blaring in the background. Or that you write better after a Frappuccino.

Everyone has at least one PAT. Discover yours and use it to your advantage.

2. <u>Keep Office Hours.</u>

The work you're doing on your personal goals and your dreams are more important than going to your day job, right? Then why don't you give them the same kind of structure? Because someone is telling you to show up at your day job? Well it's time you tell yourself to show up for your DREAM job!

Schedule a time for you to write, create, or work on your action items. From 8 – 10 PM, or during lunch from 12 – 1 PM. Or just on weekends. And I know, we're all busy and it's hard to find the time to do this. But I'm not asking for a full eight-hour day or even a four-hour day. If you can only do 30 minutes, then hey, that's a start!!! Shoot, I'm writing this chapter at 1:22 AM on a Monday night (or rather Tuesday morning).

Get into the habit of working on your goals at the same time every day or week. The schedule and structure will, without a doubt, help you accomplish your goals faster.

Check out the bestselling *The Other 8 Hours* by Robert Pagliarini for tips on how to work around your day job.

3.   Reward Yourself.

This is a fun one.

Set your daily goal, or your weekly goal, and then (here's the fun part) give yourself a big ol' juicy reward when you reach that goal. It can be your favorite ice cream, a massage...or try this...pay yourself! Literally!

Take $20, or $50 or whatever amount you want and put it aside when you accomplish your goal for the week, like a salary. And then, blow it on the weekend like a high school kid who just got his first paycheck, or save it for a trip you've wanted to take. Like "office hours," this is a great way to make your passion feel like an occupation instead of a hobby.

4. Go Public.

Want some accountability? Tell the world what you want to do.

It has been proven time and time again that if you write a goal down or say it out loud, you are much more likely to accomplish that goal. And when those goals are shared with other people, you are much more likely to do that goal.

So put your goals on Facebook, Twitter, or your own blog. If social media isn't your thing, announce it to your family at the dinner table. You won't want to disappoint those people so you're more likely to come through. And, since the people you'll be talking to (online or off) should be your friends and connections, they'll be more likely to support you through your process. So tell the world you want to lose 10 lbs, or that you are going to finish your play in three months, etc.

TIP

Public announcements are great for fitness goals (losing weight, running a marathon), since they can be so specific. And putting it out there that you want to accomplish something makes you very accountable.

And if this isn't enough to keep you on track, then maybe you should...

5. Ask For Help.

Here's a dirty secret of our educational system. The teachers you had in high school, and even in college, weren't standing in front of you because they were smarter than you.

Sure, they might have known something you didn't. But the other big reason that you had a teacher...was just to make sure you finished DOING YOUR @#$%!

They made you do your homework. They gave you tests. They gave you grades! Without these teachers, how far do you think you would have gone through the educational system? If your education was left to your own devices, do you think you would have made it?

So why, oh, why do we ever expect to accomplish anything in life without help?

It's like working out.

I hate the gym. HATE it. But with a trainer, not only do I train smarter, I am much more likely to show up, because first, I'm paying him, and second, there's an appointment in my calendar that says I'm supposed to show up (see Office Hours section!).

So get a coach, a trainer, a consultant, or just a friend (having a "Goal Buddy" who you have to check in with and "show your work" on each action item you create is super helpful). Attend classes, go to workshops...whatever you need to do to make sure you are held accountable for your actions.

Tip

In *Think and Grow Rich,* you'll read about Napoleon Hill's mastermind concept. After you read this section, go join one, or start one right away.

Everybody needs a little help now and then. I've been seeing the same "coach" for almost 20 years now. And there's no question that she is responsible for many of the things that have gone well in my life, personally to professionally.

Sure, I've paid her a lot of money in those 20 years. But she's helped me make a lot more money, and achieve some things that are priceless. The right coach is the best investment you can make in your success. Because the return on your investment can be so extraordinary monetarily, and in terms of your happiness.

Remember, getting stuck happens to ALL of us, including me.

Some days I stare at my To-Do list...I stare at my Action Items...and some piston in my brain doesn't fire. And I sit there, actionless, wanting to surf the web and watch cat videos.

For whatever reason, I just stall.

But now I know how to shake that cat-video feeling and get myself unstuck and actioning @#$% again, to make sure that I don't lose the momentum we talked about in Chapter Four.

Use some of the examples above if they work for you.

But I also encourage you to find your own. Keep experimenting...and you will find your way out of The Dip. And that little thing...the right reward...the right music...the right whatever...will be the key to restarting your action engine.

CONCLUSION

"THIS IS NOT THE END. THIS IS YOUR BEGINNING."
- KEN DAVENPORT

The method I've described in this book is simple. And it's not a "secret." It's the same way the printing press was invented, how we put a man on the moon, and what got me to where I am today.

And what's going to get me where I'm going, because I'm not done yet. Not by half.

And if it can do all the things I've done, I promise you can too.

Because I'm not the smartest guy around. Or the most talented. I just figured out a method to make stuff happen.

But this method is an idea. It's a thought that I've just written down and served over to you, like that tennis ball.

Remember, without action, that idea...this idea...is worthless. Without a response from you, the ball dribbles off to a corner of the court.

It's your responsibility, if you want success, and if you want it *badly*, to action this idea. It's your responsibility to hit the ball back over the net. No one is going to do it for you. And hey, even if they did, I promise you it wouldn't be half as good.

I know you were hoping and dreaming that this conclusion would include a magic shortcut to success. Sorry. No such luck. That's why this book probably won't sell a billion copies. Because the truth ain't easy to swallow.

<u>There are no shortcuts to success.</u>

You find success by taking action. A small action at first. (Hey, picking up this book was an action.) And then taking more action. And more. And more, until you're spent.

And then you take more action.

That's how you cure cancer, write a Pulitzer Prize-winning play, or, hey, even write a book like this one.

It's by taking **ACTION**.

You got it now, right?

So then...what are you waiting for?

ONE FINAL THOUGHT

"THE WAY TO GET STARTED IS TO QUIT TALKING AND GET DOING."
- WALT DISNEY

Before you close this book, do one final exercise for me.

See the space below? Write the ONE action item (keep it small, keep it easy) that you ARE going to do tomorrow to help you get closer to your goal. (Do you like how I gave you today off? I figured finishing the book was your action item for today – but hey, don't hesitate to overachieve/overaction and do something today too.)

Ready?

Write it here:

I am going to

_____.

Now. Go do it. And then the next day, do this exercise again.

And then do it again, and ...

Q&A From Ken's Live Seminar

The following is a transcript from the Q&A portion of Ken's live "ACTION!" seminar, which was taught on Tuesday, February 23rd, 2016.

Debbie: Hi there.

Ken: Hi.

Debbie: Hi, this is Debbie. Hi, Ken, thank you. Are you ready for my question now?

Ken: I am ready for your question. Where are you calling from, first?

Debbie: I'm calling from the Boston area.

Ken: Go Red Sox!

Debbie: Okay, great. Not really.

Ken: Shoot.

Debbie: When I start something, it does seem to snowball, and the problem that I've experienced is I get quickly overwhelmed and I feel like I have obligations, I'm behind this thing, and then I often run into some technical problems that put me even further behind. So what's a good thing to do when things are moving very fast and then you get overblown by them?

Ken: This is one of those asset/liability problems. It's fantastic because you've done all of this stuff, you've gotten going and things are happening and now you've got to sort through it all. It's a challenge and it happens to me all of the time because I have a number of projects going at once so I need to keep them all very, very organized as I do.

The first thing to remember is, look, all of us on this call, we all want to achieve great things, we're probably all a little impatient and we probably want things to happen tomorrow. I am one of them...hello, my hand is raised, it's very, very high right now...but I will tell you this: there is no timeline.

One of the most important things that I do when I'm getting a little overwhelmed and I'm staring at my inbox and there are 25 things to do...for example, I told you how I can't have my desk with stuff on it, I also can't have my inbox with any e-mail in it by the end of the day. I have to have them all done or I can't go to sleep. It's one of my rules for myself but it's also one of the things that keep me on point. So it can be overwhelming.

I can see out of the corner of my eye my email inbox blowing up right now and that's going to be a little frightening for me, it's going to be a late night for me, but one of the things I do when I'm working on a project like this and you've got ten tasks is slow yourself down, take a breath, you've hired yourself.

Remember, you're your own employee. It's okay to slow that employee down because it's actually more important that you slow it down and you do everything right than do everything super-fast.

So the point is to keep action going, the point is not to keep action going to the point where you are speeding down the highway and careening off the road. So the biggest piece of advice I can give to you is, as it's coming in, slow things down a little bit. Slow things down, sort through the stuff that you've got to do, prioritize it, take those ten things that you have to do, prioritize it to a top ten list.

Another reason Toodledo is great is because it does actually prioritize for you what's the first thing, and start there. Slowly but surely get yourself through it. Okay, thanks for that question, Debbie from Boston, and let's see if we have any other questions.

Max: Hi, Ken.

Ken: Yes, hi, go ahead.

Max: My name is Max M., I'm calling from New York.

Ken: Hi, Max. Welcome, go ahead with your question.

Max Well right now I'm creating a project, it's the first time ever I've been the leader of a project idea. A lot of things you have to prepare for, to take action, like you said, but I'm right now at a roadblock that is basically, of course, the money issue, and I feel like sometimes I get a lot of fear of what to do and it has been now three weeks since I have advanced in that. I would like to know, for example, in your life, when you first started, were you ever fearful when you were starting to produce?

Ken: Absolutely, and I will tell you this right now...I am afraid every single day. I am afraid every single day. There is an element of fear many times during the day but certainly when I just started, certainly.

The first thing to know, for all of you who are dealing with this, it's okay, it's fine. In fact I'll give you a couple of quotes. Tiger Woods was once asked about whether he got nervous when he got on the first tee of a golf tournament and I think they expected him to say that he didn't get nervous and he said, "I am nervous every single time I step up there. The day I am not nervous, the day I am not a little scared, is the day I give it up."

He knew that fear, that energy, actually, can be translated into good. It's that feeling that's showing that you're actually doing something.

The other one is they did a study on this, they studied a whole bunch of very, very successful business people and they asked them the question, "How did you conquer fear? How did you do that? Because it takes a lot to do what you do."

Whether that's brain surgery, whether that's starting a brand new company, whether that's Uber taking on the city of New York and trying to get a presence here, and what they found out was that these CEOs all said the same thing.

They all said that it wasn't that they didn't have any fear, it was that when they feared something that was exactly when they knew they had to do it, whatever it was. If they feared asking people for money, they asked someone for money, because the moment you do, you've conquered the fear. You've conquered it. The challenge, and I'm so glad you asked this question, because the hard part is fear can be paralyzing and in the span of three weeks you haven't done anything, just based on that fear.

Of course one of the questions you should ask yourself is how to get into that fear and break it apart. What's the worst thing that can happen to you if you ask someone for money? They could say "No." That's it.

I will tell you, I have asked thousands of people for money, no one has ever laughed at me. And even if they laugh at me, so what? No one's ever punched me in the face either and, frankly, even if someone punched me in the face, well they've punched me in the face, I would probably sue them and get money from them anyway. So what's the worst thing that could happen to you?

You've got to ask that question and then you've got to figure out a way to break through the fear and that's why I teach this system, that's why I've talked about everything, because you know what isn't emotional? Action.

I wrote a book about raising money. If you're interested in

that it's called *Raise It* and it's available at TheProducersPerspective.com. But part of the whole system of raising money is based on this system of action.

First step, develop a list of leads. Second step, contact leads. It is just action items. We want to remove the emotion out of you, pull it out, we want to get you operating like an action machine. You're on an assembly line and all you do is action, action, action. You're like these telemarketers that pick up the phone and dial, dial, dial and ask and they operate on a script, and actually that can help you too.

Emotion gets into things when we are unsure of what to do next. Write yourself a script. You know what the most successful script I ever wrote was?

When I was 13, 14 years old I asked the first girl I was ever going to ask out on a date, I asked her out on a date, you know what I did? I wrote a script for it because I tried to ask the same girl out like a week ago and I blubbered all over myself and made an idiot out of myself but the next time I wrote a script and called her up and I at least got the question out and she did say yes. The date was a disaster but she did say yes.

So the point is we want to remove the emotion out of it, we want to put a script into place, things that, again, make your path seem like picking up the dry cleaning. So what I want you to do tonight is what's one small thing you can do? Tomorrow, ask someone, call someone, develop a lead, whatever it is. Don't think about the fear and just drive through the action. Okay, next question.

Jessica: Hi, Ken. My name's Jessica.

Ken: Hi, Jessica. Where are you calling from?

Jessica: I'm calling from Minneapolis.

Ken: I love Minneapolis. Shoot with your question.

Jessica: Well my question is, this is all great information, however there are, particularly in the arts, there's a lot of things, specifically in auditioning, when things are not in your control, as it were, so my question is what you would do with things, how do I put this, if you can lose the part to the fact that you're too tall, too thin, look like the director's ex-wife, and I'm just wondering if there's a way to combat that and if there's an action oriented path that does it.

Ken: Absolutely. Look, the thing is, sometimes when you serve the tennis ball, like you go in for whatever role that you want to play, the other person doesn't hit it back to you.

Now, this is why, for artists and entrepreneurs, especially at the beginning of their careers, you have to serve a lot of tennis balls. You have to send out more inquiry emails, you have to audition a thousand times more than someone who is more established. As you're getting started...and unfortunately getting started doesn't just mean your first day on the job, it could mean until you've achieved a certain number of credits and it could mean, for some, until the middle of your career.

Unfortunately, in a highly competitive industry like acting, writing, etc., you've got to serve a lot of tennis balls, you've got to get out there and audition more.

The action part of what I'm talking about here with you is

that, look, sometimes someone doesn't want to play ball with you. I could give you 10 to 20 things that I wanted to produce that would make fantastic musicals. Books, movies, you name it, I've got it and people have said no, in the same way that they would say, like you said, "Oh, you're too tall," or "We want a blonde for this role," or whatever it is.

It's not in my control either if some estate never wants a musical of, I don't know, To Kill a Mockingbird, let's just say. That's not in my control either, so it's not just performing, it's in everything.

What is in my control is to serve a tennis ball to someone else. What is in my control is to control the things I can control, which are, for performers, again, auditioning for a thousand other things, it's coming up with a show of your own, it's creating a YouTube channel that shows, if someone says, "We need someone funnier," well you create a YouTube channel that shows that you are funny.

The great thing about the world we live in now, the DIY world we live in now, is you can actually do so much more for yourself as a performer than you ever could, even when people tell you, "You don't belong in this show." It's going to happen.

People tell me this all the time. "Ken, we don't want you to have the rights to this show." They say this to me raising money. "Ken, I don't want to invest in your show." Well, what do I do? Unfortunately, at some point, that's out of my control, so I ask other people.

So for you specifically it's about getting out there, it's about auditioning for more things, serving more tennis balls, and then, hey, I can tell, you're on this call, and the question you asked, you don't like when you can't control things, so what can you do, at the same time that you're auditioning for these shows, what can you do that is in your control?

What can you do tomorrow? Could you write your own play? Could you produce one? Could you, again, create a different, unique character, like Miranda Sings? Look what happened with Miranda Sings. If you don't know about Miranda Sings, Google that. Control the things you can control. Okay, let's take another question.

Question: Hi, Ken.

Ken: Hi there. Speak up, I can't hear you very well.

Question: Can you hear me now?

Ken: Yeah, even louder though, go for it.

Question: Okay, my question for you is how do you go about, the idea part I get, I get that you have ideas and ideas and ideas, but how do you go about inquiring . . .

Ken: I'm having real trouble hearing you. Say the last part. I know it's about ideas, how do you what with the ideas?

Question: How do you maintain the enthusiasm?

Ken: How do you retain the enthusiasm for your idea?

Question: Yeah, with other people.

Ken: Oh, how do you make sure other people are as enthusiastic as you are about your idea?

Question: Yes.

Ken: Okay. That is a great challenge, of course. First of all, you want to surround yourself with people that are enthusiastic from the get-go. Attract people to you and talk to people and bring them on to your project that are enthusiastic.

But listen, I've got some bad news for you, and this was something that, man, oh, man, was a tough thing for me to learn early on in my career. No one will ever be as enthusiastic about your idea as you. It's just never going to happen.

So one of the things that I do is remind myself that that's going to happen, that I'm going to get into a situation where people are not going to be as enthusiastic and when I'm saying, "Hey, I want to work 'til 6am!" people are like, "Ken, eff you, I want to go to sleep." That's going to happen, so make sure you manage your expectations first.

Understand that this is your idea, this is the project that you started, you're getting going, and people are not going to want to jump in as deep as you are in. That's the first step to this, is just realizing, and once you're a little bit more forgiving of that you can actually have more fun with it and keep them enthused about it, but that is the first step of it.

And the second part of it is, when we want to accomplish things in life, things are very high stakes for us, right? For entrepreneurs like us, for ambitious people, "I want to win a Tony Award, I want to write a show, I've got to produce this thing," it becomes this thing and one of the things that drives people away the most is when people are too fanatical and they become so driven they become obsessive about it.

Backing off just a little bit makes it a lot more fun. Taking some of the pressure off yourself and saying, "Hey, I'm just going to do this. I don't know what it's going to become, I'm just doing something. I am, action after action, going to create something and hopefully it's going to be a big hit and maybe it will be *Hamilton* and maybe not."

Taking the pressure off yourself will actually allow there to be more positive energy throughout the whole experience. I think we have one more question. Let's take one more question before we go. Thanks to everybody for staying on the line for extra time. One more question and then a quick wrap up.

Rich: Hey, Ken.

Ken: Go for it.

Rich: This is Rich from Orlando.

Ken: Hey, Rich from Orlando. Go ahead.

Rich: I am a playwright and director and I have worked for a long time in this particular area to make a name for myself but I've always worked to try to get my work farther up field, as it were, and I've been in development and won awards, etc., etc. But what would action items be from you, being in Orlando, away from the cultural hub, trying to make that impression, to get the work seen in the right hands so that it can flourish and farther?

Ken: Great, so you're a playwright in Orlando and what you're trying to do is get out of the Orlando area, right?

Rich: Yeah.

Ken: You're trying to get your work showcased in New York, perhaps, seen in other places.

Rich: Absolutely.

Ken: Great, okay. We could be on this phone for hours. I could give you a thousand of them. One of the first things is, do you have a website for yourself as a writer? Every writer out there...if there are writers listening in right now...every single writer needs to have a website promoting their stuff.

You said specifically, "I want to get my work out of Orlando."

You know what that means? You've got to get yourself out of Orlando. It doesn't mean you've got to move outside of Orlando, but every so often it means you've got to get yourself out of Orlando.

I would, tomorrow action item, I would say book a trip to New York but I'm not going to say that. You know why? Because that's actually a big commitment. There's money, there's time, there's all of these things that are like, "Oof, that's a big deal," so in detailing the system I'm teaching tonight, here's what I want you to do tomorrow. When can you come to New York?

Pick some dates three months from now, "I can go this weekend." Okay, action item one done. Next day, look for flights. "Can I afford them?" No? Look for a bus. "Where can I stay?" All of these things, one after another. Try to pick a time. Come here to New York when you can network with other playwrights, when there's a Fringe Festival going on, when the Fringe Festival is in town, so you can see other emerging developing playwrights just like you.

The other thing I would do - I would apply to the Fringe Festival, send a play in. I am a huge believer in submitting to festivals and contests for playwrights, you know why? It is such an easy way to serve a tennis ball. Such an easy way to serve it.

Take a play...you're a playwright, you've written them...take a play, put it in an envelope, follow the instructions on the Fringe Festival website, send it in. The fact is that their deadline just passed but call them...never hurts...call them and see if they'll take just one late submission. That's you serving the tennis ball.

Here's the problem...I'm so glad you asked this question and this is the last question we'll answer...a lot of people say to me, when I tell them to submit to the Fringe or submit to the New York Musical Theater Festival or submit to this contest, they say, "Ken, I don't know how to produce a show at the Fringe Festival!"

I don't care, that's not what this simple action item is about. The simple action item is only this - submit to the Fringe Festival. Serve the tennis ball and see if they hit it back. If they hit it back, we'll figure out what to do then.

Then you'll say, "Oh, am I going to accept this?" Accept. "Oh, I have to go there, I have to produce, I have to find a director."

One action item after another, but don't scare yourself, going back to the fear, into not doing the action. I could literally go on with tons of action items for you on how to get yourself out of the Orlando area, including getting yourself even more active in the Orlando area in order to do it. There are a lot of things you could do.

There are lots of clients of mine who are writers from all over and the great thing is we live in 2016. Heck, you could pretend you live in New York and live in Orlando and be a successful writer. So thank you very much for that question.

Now, one more thing before you go. Before you go, do me a favor. Take out a piece of paper, open up a blank document in your Microsoft Word or whatever it is. I will wait, go ahead. Now ask yourself this question: What's one thing that you can do to get yourself closer to what you dream about doing? Now, remember mine. Remember it? How many people remember what my first action item was?

If you said posting the audition notice for *The Awesome 80s Prom* you would actually be wrong. It was a trick question, I gotcha. The one action item that I did that is responsible for me being here tonight in front of you? It was my letter to Hal Prince.

That was the first domino to my career, a letter. Me sitting down and writing a fan boy letter to my favorite director, saying, "I want to do what you do." That's it. I would not be here if it wasn't for that one letter. That's how small these action items can be, but they can lead to huge things.

So ask yourself, what will yours be? What's the one action item, the one small thing you can do tomorrow to start the domino effect on your career? Maybe it's that you ask for the rights to that movie, like I talked about, or, again, maybe it's just getting the address for the movie company. I don't care how small the action item is - I want it to be small - come up with one right now and write it down. Got it? Good.

Now tomorrow, not tonight...you've listened in tonight so that's your action item for the day...tomorrow, do that one thing. Just do it, and then tomorrow night come up with another action item, and then the next day do that. I guarantee you just one thing a day, simple action items compounding up themselves, I guarantee you will achieve exactly what you want to before you know it, and when you do, you'll be like me, sitting in my office right now with a Tony

Award looming over my head, the plaques on the wall and a list of Broadway shows that are coming up over the next several years.

It will be like, "Huh, I don't even realize how I got here." I promise it will happen, as long as you just keep actioning items. So did you write it down? You wrote down one? Got it? Good. Now go take action.

KEN'S RECOMMENDED READING

Think and Grow Rich by Napoleon Hill

Do the Work: Overcome Resistance and Get Out of Your Own Way by Steven Pressfield

The Dip by Seth Godin

The Other 8 Hours: Maximize Your Free Time to Create New Wealth & Purpose by Robert Pagliarini

The Secret by Rhonda Byrne

About the Author

Ken is a Tony Award-winning Broadway and Off Broadway Producer. Broadway: *Groundhog Day*, *The Play That Goes Wrong*, *Spring Awakening* (Tony nomination), *It's Only a Play*, *Macbeth* starring Alan Cumming, *Godspell*, *Kinky Boots* (Broadway - Tony Award, National Tour, Toronto, Australia, and West End), *The Visit* (Tony nomination), *Mothers and Sons* (Tony nomination), *The Bridges of Madison County* (National Tour), *Allegiance*, *Chinglish*, *Oleanna* starring Bill Pullman and Julia Stiles, *Speed-the-Plow*, Will Ferrell's *You're Welcome America* (Tony nomination), *Blithe Spirit* (Broadway, West End and National Tour), and *13*.

Off-Broadway: *Daddy Long Legs*, *Altar Boyz* (Co-

Conceiver), *My First Time* (Author), *The Awesome 80s Prom* (Creator), and *Miss Abigail's Guide to Dating, Mating, & Marriage* (Author). Ken's productions have been produced internationally in over 25 countries.

Ken is also the Executive Producer for North America for Andrew Lloyd Webber's Really Useful Group.

Ken's unique style has garnered him two front page articles in the *NY Times*, features on MSNBC, Rock Center, Fox News, BBC, and a mention in Jay Leno's monologue on "The Tonight Show." Ken was named one of *Crain's* "40 Under Forty," and is one of the co-founders of TEDxBroadway. Other projects include: smartphone app Did He Like It™ , Broadway board game *Be A Broadway Star*. His blog, TheProducersPerspective.com, has been featured in *Vanity Fair*, *New York Magazine*, *The Gothamist*, and more.

Upcoming projects include his original musical *Gettin' The Band Back Together* (George Street Playhouse premiere), the new play *Do This*, and revivals of *Once on This Island*, *The Great White Hope*, and *Mass Appeal*, as well as the movie, *Band Dorks*.

OTHER BOOKS BY THE AUTHOR

*Producing 101: The Three Fundamentals
of Producing Theater*

Raise It: How to Raise Millions for Your Show and Fast

Breakin' Down a Broadway Budget

Make Your Mark with Your Marketing

For a full list of books and products by Ken Davenport, visit:

www.TheProducersPerspective.com/store

Feeling Alone in Your Pursuit of Success?

You're not alone in feeling alone.

Twenty years ago, I was just a guy with a bunch of ideas, and a dream of getting them up on a stage. But how?

I searched everywhere I could from the library to the chat rooms of America Online, and I couldn't find any answers to my burning questions, from how to raise money for a show, to what a Broadway budget looked like and so many more.

So, I spent the next ten years of my life working my way up on Broadway, so I could figure out the fastest and most efficient way to get a show to the stage...and give it the best chance to succeed.

And I vowed that once I gained that knowledge, I'd share it with others, so they could use it to get help to pursue their

Broadway and Off Broadway dreams. Because I had this feeling that there were a lot of other people out there, all over the world, who were just like me.

That's why I created The Producer's Perspective PRO, the only site of its kind, dedicated to helping you get your show off the ground...and fast.

So whether you're a writer, producer, director or just a fan, I hope you'll join me, and the many others who have joined our PRO community. Because we're making stuff happen. And I want that for you, too.

And trust me, it can happen.

THE PRODUCER'S PERSPECTIVE PRO

A BROADWAY PRODUCER'S OPINION ON EVERYTHING BROADWAY AND BEYOND

- ✔ **FREE Monthly Webinars**
- ✔ **Monthly Newsletter**
- ✔ **Vendor Resource Lists**
- ✔ **Sample Document Library**
- ✔ **Bonus Package Worth $347!**

JOIN PRO TODAY!

www.TheProducersPerspective.com/join

"PRO equips you with the resources necessary to take your career to the next level." – Jeremy D.

"The reason to join PRO is to get an insider's perspective and to have a friendly insider--Ken--who is on your side and helping you." – Elizabeth S.

"PRO gave us the feeling of being able to talk about our project with confidence, as well as being able to ask questions of others who are going through a similar experience and being able to sort of trade and share information. " – Charles Y.

"If you feel like it's too hard, Ken makes it feel pretty easy." – Megan K.

"Very often when you're dealing with people who are in the Broadway community, they use terms that people outside the community might not understand... One of the webinars on PRO described what we needed to know if we intend to produce shows. This is all part of our vocabulary and this is all part of our experience and we need to be a little more savvy about it."– Nancy P.